The Dysgraphia Sourcebook: Everything You Need to Help Your Child

Ben Bryce, MAT, Bill Stephens MD (Ed.)

ISBN 978-1499612752

Contents

Introduction 5

Signs of Dysgraphia 6

Types of Dysgraphia 12

Treatment 17

    Specific Strategies: 26

Spatial Dysgraphia...26

Motor Dysgraphia 30

Dyslexic Dysgraphia 40

    For-Fee Products...43

    Free Products 45

Related Disorders...53

Appendix 81

Glossary..97

References 103

Index...115

Introduction

Dysgraphia is a learning disability that affects the ability to write. It is different from an intellectual disability. A person with an intellectual disability has limitations with mental functioning and in skills like communication or taking care of themselves; people of normal intelligence have dysgraphia in spite of normal intelligence. However, dysgraphia often overlaps with other learning disabilities like speech impairment, attention deficit disorder or developmental coordination disorder.

Although a fairly uncommon disorder, many famous people have dysgraphia including the author Agatha Christie, American General George Patton, actor and director Henry Winkler and the scientist Thomas Edison.

The word dysgraphia is derived from Greek:
Dys = impaired
Graph = "writing by hand".

Signs of Dysgraphia

The general signs of dysgraphia differ according to which type of dysgraphia your child has. A low self-esteem is common for all ages. Your child may have some, or all of the following symptoms:

Ages 4-6

- Cramped or unusual pencil grip
- Problems with learning the alphabet, including the inability to learn the letters in their name
- A dislike of writing and/or drawing
- Avoidance or poor performance of fine motor skills, like drawing or holding a pencil, painting or cutting with scissors
- Frustration with drawing or writing
- Inability to compose their own words (copying may be okay)

Ages 7-12

- Talking to oneself when writing
- Watching their hand when writing

- Cramped or unusual pencil grip
- Strange paper position or body/wrist position
- Unfinished words or omitted words
- Poor spelling
- Illegible handwriting
- Poor spacing between words
- Mixing of upper case and lower case letters
- Getting tired easily of writing
- Slow, labored writing or copying (even if the writing is legible)

Teens and Adults

- Watching their hand when writing
- Talking to oneself when writing
- Cramped or unusual pencil grip
- Strange paper position or body/wrist position
- Mixing print and cursive writing
- Poor organization of writing ideas
- Difficulty with main ideas and supporting sentences
- Avoiding writing
- Noticeable gap between speech and written work
- Taking a long time to complete written word assignments
- Problems with spelling and grammar
- Slow, labored writing or copying (even if the writing is legible)

Diagnosis

Dysgraphia cannot be diagnosed just by looking at a handwriting sample. A qualified clinician, like an occupational therapist, must directly test your child. The test will include writing sentences and paragraphs and copying age-appropriate writing. The clinician doesn't just look at the finished handwriting sample; they will also look at *how* your child writes. This includes:

- Posture
- Position
- Pencil grip
- Fatigue
- Cramping
- Tremor of the writing hand
- Hand-eye coordination

The examiner might also check fine-motor speed by asking your child to tap their fingers and turn their wrists.

What Causes Dysgraphia?

English is one of the world's most complex languages to learn how to read and write. The complexity of a language's orthography is directly linked to how difficult it is to learn to read that language.

An orthography is the way language is written. It includes the rules for spelling, grammar, punctuation, hyphenation, word breaks and capitalization. If a language sounds like it is spelled, it's easier to read than languages with complex rules. English has a deep orthographic structure with spelling patterns at several different levels like letter-sound correspondences, syllables, and morphemes (the smallest grammatical unit in a language). Almost every letter in English can be sounded more than one way (think of how many ways you can pronounce the letter "e"). In comparison, languages like Spanish and Finnish are spelled how they sound, making them easier to learn to read and write.

Different types of writing systems (e.g., alphabetic as compared to logographic writing systems found in Japanese and Chinese systems) require different parts of the brain in order to read, write, and spell. Therefore, children with reading problems in one language might not have one in a language with another orthography.

Current research suggests that dysgraphia is caused by problems with orthographic coding in working memory. Orthographic coding refers to the ability to store unfamiliar written words (along with the language rules) in temporary or permanent memory. Coding of orthographic information is the "ability to represent the unique array of letters that defines a printed word, as well as general attributes of the writing system such as sequential dependencies, structural redundancies, letter position frequencies, and so forth" (Vellutino, Scanlon & Tanzman, 1994, p. 314). Put like that, you can see that writing a single word on a piece of paper to represent something is a complex process.

Dysgraphia is also in part due to underlying problems in the orthographic loop and graphomotor output. The orthographic loop of working memory integrates the letters and written words in the mind's eye with hand and finger movements needed for writing.

Development of orthographic skills is largely attributed to reading and exposure to printed words (Stanovich & West, 1989; Rayner et al., 2001). Exactly *how* this process works isn't clearly understood, but what is known is that repeated exposure to letters and words allows the brain to see patterns and store words and letters. If you have dysgraphia, the brain's inability to store the words and letters as pictures means that you have trouble remembering and writing those words.

Some research suggests that dysgraphia may be a hereditary condition. Several studies have shown strong evidence for a biological basis for dyslexia, where more research has been performed than with any other learning disability. Many studies are also looking at a genetic link for dysgraphia.

Research shows that that three kinds of specific written language disabilities –dysgraphia, dyslexia (impaired word decoding and spelling), and selective language disorder (oral and written language learning disability, OWL LD) can be diagnosed and characterized depending on which part of the working memory component is affected:

- **Dyslexia:** Spoken and written word form and syntactic storage (storage of syntax of words) and processing units.
- **Dysgraphia:** Phonological (the part of the brain that deals with sound or phonological information) and orthographic loops (the part of the brain that deals with the method for writing a language).
- **OWL LD:** Supervisory attention/executive functions like selective attention, attention switching, and sustained attention.

Each working memory component is thought to be associated with different genes (Berninger and Richards, 2010). The earliest evidence that dyslexia is genetic or "runs in the family" dates from the early 1900s (Hinshelwood, 1907; Stephenson, 1907). At the time of writing, it is thought that, like dyslexia, dysgraphia runs in families. However, the specific genes that may be responsible for dysgraphia have not been identified.

Types of Dysgraphia

There are three types of dysgraphia:

1. Dyslexic Dysgraphia

A person with dyslexic dysgraphia (sometimes called processing dysgraphia) can copy text, color and draw close to normal. However, spelling words out loud (oral spelling) is below age level and written text is illegible (unreadable). This type of dyslexia is caused by issues with the orthographic loop. The orthographic loop helps with temporary memory and permanent memorization of words and letters. People with processing dysgraphia have trouble forming images in their head or forming words and letters in their mind's eye.

2. Motor Dysgraphia

A person with motor dysgraphia can color, draw and paint within normal boundaries but has trouble with all written work, included copied work. They may also have trouble with other fine motor skills like opening water bottles, manipulating pencils, or tying shoes. Motor dysgraphia is caused by poor fine motor skills.

3. Spatial dysgraphia

Drawing, coloring and painting are always below normal with spatial dysgraphia. Handwriting is illegible with unevenly spaced and sized letters. This type of dysgraphia is caused by the brain having problems with evaluating what the eyes are seeing and how objects are positioned relative to each other.

Each of the three types has a different treatment option, so it's vital you find out which type of dysgraphia you or your child has. It's possible to have more than one type, or even all three at the same time. An occupational therapist who is experienced with learning disabilities can determine if you or your child has motor dysgraphia, although it can be a little trickier to differentiate between processing and spatial dysgraphia. Talk with your school district's special education department to find out what options are available to you for diagnosing learning disabilities; some districts employ qualified clinicians who can diagnose dysgraphia. You can also talk with your family physician, who may know of a specialist near you. A team of professionals is usually required to diagnose dysgraphia, but some individuals with a background in psychology, language and education may be qualified to make a diagnosis. Some of the professionals you may encounter are:

Clinical Psychologist
Clinical Psychologists assess, diagnose, treat and prevent mental disorders. Within the field of clinical psychology, there are many sub-specialties including child mental health, emotional substances and learning disabilities. If you decide to look for a

clinical psychologist to evaluate your child, make sure they specialize in learning disabilities.

School Psychological Examiners

School Psychological Examiners are assessors who work with students in public schools, interviewing, observing, and administering and interpreting standardized testing instruments that measure cognitive and academic abilities. They determine eligibility for special education services and placement, and also provide occupational guidance and planning.

Occupational Therapist

The role of an occupational therapist is to work with a client to help them achieve a fulfilled and satisfied state in life through the use of "purposeful activity or interventions designed to achieve functional outcomes which promote health, prevent injury or disability and which develop, improve, sustain or restore the highest possible level of independence"(AOTA). Occupational therapists may work exclusively with children with learning disabilities and sometimes work as an employee within school districts to provide occupational therapy.

Assistive Technology Specialist

Assistive technology specialists provide service to help people with disabilities choose and use assistive technology devices like specialized computer software. They evaluate a person's needs, and help the person to acquire and use the assistive technology product. School districts often employ assistive technology specialists as an integral part of their special education programs.

Special Education Teacher

A special education teacher educates children with special needs like learning disabilities. Children with learning disabilities usually are referred to special education services when their regular classroom teacher notices that the child with normal intelligence is not performing at their expected level.

In the United States, Canada and UK, an IEP (Individualized Education Plan) may be used to plan special education for your child. In the United States, Another plan called a 504 plan is often used for students with dysgraphia.

What is an IEP?

The IEP is a program that ensures a school child with an identified disability under the law receives specialized education services such as occupational therapy. The Individuals with Disabilities Education Act (IDEA) requires your child to have one of the 13 disabilities listed in the act and that they need special education services to progress in school. In addition to having a learning disability, your child used to have to be performing 1.5 to 2 levels behind grade level in order to qualify for special education services. However, a recent update in IDEA means that any child who needs help can receive it. This makes sense; before the change in IDEA, a child at risk had first have to fall behind before receiving services. Now, the goal is prevention as well as remediation.

What is a 504?

Another term you may hear is a 504 plan. It's a reference to Section 504 of the Rehabilitation Act of 1973. Schools that receive federal funding must offer 504 plans. This plan is also for school children who have a disability defined by law. The main difference is that with a 504 plan, students don't require specialized instruction and do not have to be performing below grade level. The 504 plans are also easier to get than an IEP. In general, if your child is diagnosed with dysgraphia, either by a school psychologist or outside professional, that's generally all they need to receive 504 accommodations. Your school may also offer informal instruction and accommodations like frequent breaks or longer test taking times. It is a good plan if a student is identified as having dysgraphia but does not meet the legal requirements of the Individuals with Disabilities Act.

What this means for Dysgraphia

In general, an IEP is harder to get than a 504. An IEP gets you services and accommodations, while a 504 only gets you the accommodations. A lot depends on how severe your child's dysgraphia is, and how far behind in school they are. However, in most cases a 504 plan will be sufficient for helping your child.

Treatment

General Modifications and Accommodations

Each of the three types of dysgraphia has a slightly different course of treatment. However, there are some modifications and accommodations you and the school can make for *any* type of dysgraphia:

Teach the Alphabet Differently

When your child is learning the alphabet, have them repeat this process for each letter:

1. Study the letter.
2. Name the letter.
3. Cover the letter and try to visualize it in the mind's eye.
4. Write the letter from memory.
5. Compare what they have written to the actual letter.

Following these steps will help a child with dysgraphia remember the letters. Naming the letters of the alphabet when learning uses another part of the brain called the *phonological loop*, which has to do with sounds. Using another part of the brain in addition to the orthographic loop can help your child overcome dysgraphia.

Handwriting Tips

Allow your child to use whatever style of handwriting they feel most comfortable with (i.e. script or cursive writing). For some children with dysgraphia, cursive writing is actually preferable. Cursive writing eliminates the need to remove the pencil from the paper and figure out word spacing or where to place the pencil back down to start the next letter. Cursive writing also has fewer possibilities for reversing letters. Surprisingly, children with dysgraphia may actually benefit from learning cursive right off the bat, instead of struggling with the spacing and placement problems of block letter writing. Cursive writing also differentiates letters a lot better than script. Take the letters b, d, p, and q:

b d p q

The "b" looks like a backwards "d" and the "p" looks like a flipped q. In cursive, the letters look a lot less similar with slanted letters and tops and tails that connect the letters:

$$b\ d\ p\ q$$

Dot to Dot Letters
Encourage younger children to connect dots or dashes to make letters (see Appendix for an example work sheet). This simple tool can help your child develop muscle memory, or automatic writing of letters.

A B C D

Give Extra Time
Allow the student extra time to complete written work, including homework and tests. Ideally, the homework workload should be reduced by the teacher. For example, a regular student without dysgraphia might be expected to complete two hours of homework a night and the teacher will give the

student worksheets (perhaps two) to complete in that time frame. For a student with dysgraphia, those same worksheets might take a long, frustrating four hours or more. You don't want your child to be frustrated with work – you want them to enjoy it. Ask the teacher to reduce the workload for your child if they are spending a long time each night on homework.

Start Early

A teacher should allow the student to start an assignment or project early, to allow for extra time to complete the work. Most teachers plan out work weeks in advance (if not the entire semester). If there is a long project at some stage, the teacher should let a student with dysgraphia know well in advance, to give them time to prepare a visual organizer to plan the project out.

Computing

Teach your child keyboarding skills. Keyboarding skills can help with most students with dysgraphia. It gives them an alternate form of expression without the added frustration of trying to remember how to form and print letters and words. There are many, many programs that can help your child overcome their dysgraphia. See the section in this book on Software for some suggestions.

Spell Checking

Encourage your child to use a spell checker on the computer. If your student has trouble recognizing misspelled words, there are software programs that speak the words instead of highlighting them. For example, the software *Co-Writer* offers suggestions for basic grammar and spelling; it can be integrated with the *Write Out Loud* text-to-speech program.

Prepare in Advance

Have your child prepare assignment papers in advance with the appropriate headings (name, teacher, subject, date etc.), perhaps using a computer. This knocks off one task and allows your child to concentrate on the actual assignment instead of going through the frustrating task of writing their name, date etc. which can derail their enthusiasm even before the actual assignment is started!

Alternate Assignments for Essays

Teachers can give a student with dysgraphia an alternate test if essay writing is required. For example, multiple choice tests may be more appropriate for a child with dysgraphia. Other options are oral tests or being allowed to use a computer to type the assignment.

Don't Chastise!

Avoid criticizing your child for sloppy work. Emphasize how proud you are of them for trying and find positive things to show praise for. For example, your child may have a good main idea or, despite having "sloppy" handwriting, they may have organized paragraphs. Children with dysgraphia often have poor self-esteem; show encouragement instead of making negative comments.

Encourage the Use of Visual Organizers

Encourage the student to use visual organizers for lengthier assignments. A visual organizer, also known as knowledge map, concept map, story map, cognitive organizer, advance organizer, or concept diagram, is a tool that uses visual symbols to express knowledge, concepts, thoughts, or ideas, and the relationships between them. Visual organizers can help a student keep on track with the assignment parts and complete an assignment in small steps (for example, brainstorming, main idea and spelling check).

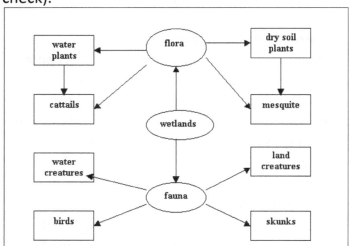

A type of concept map

What you include in a visual organizer depends on the grade level of your child. You can help your child make a visual organizer. One of the best ways is on a computer using a mind mapping software program (see the Software section in this book for suggestions).

Concept maps can be used for any age, for any subject from writing short stories to advanced math.

fig. 4: Concept Map

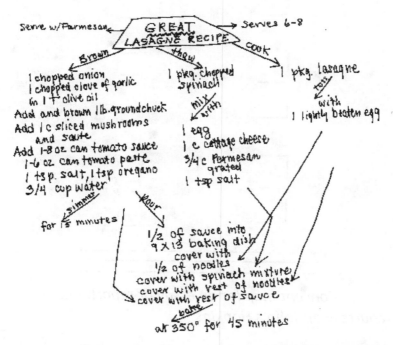

Recipe Concept Map. Image courtesy of John's Hopkins

fig. 3: Writing Chart

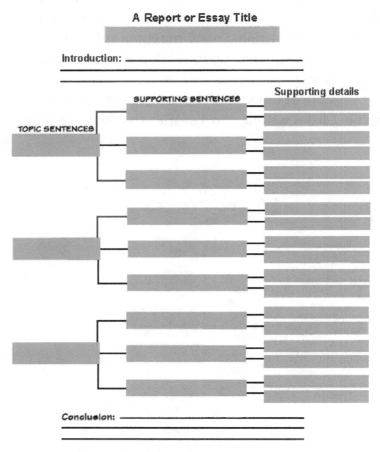

Concept map for an essay or report. Image courtesy of: John's Hopkins.

3-Ring Binders

Provide a 3-ring binder containing everything your child needs for successful writing. The binder can include a sheet on the inside cover with the letters of the alphabet, a template for the required written work format and other visual organizers.

Mazes

Mazes can be an excellent way for your child to develop fine motor control. When doing a maze, ask your child to keep the line inside the lines of the maze (in other words, the pencil line mustn't touch the edges). There are many maze books on the market that cater to all ages. We've included a few simple mazes in the Appendix.

A more complicated maze used in a geometry class. Image: Andrew's University.

Specific Strategies:

Spatial Dysgraphia

Children with spatial dysgraphia have trouble understanding space, which results in illegible written and copied work although spelling abilities are normal. They also have problems with drawing.

Treatment for spatial dysgraphia is normally part of an IEP or 504 plan. The plans outline what changes are to be made to your child's education and include what your child is expected to learn. This includes accommodations for how your child learns and is tested. These modifications and accommodations are usually necessary for your child over their entire school career because spatial dysgraphia is not likely to get better. What changes is for your child to learn to work with the condition and to develop sound study habits to help them overcome their dysgraphia as they learn.

Possible modifications depend on your child, your child's school and the school's budget. Common modifications include providing lined paper for all tasks and providing a computer or tablet for some work. To help your child at home, follow the suggestions recommended by the IEP or 504 plan. For example, if one of the recommended accommodations is the provision of lined paper or graph paper, stock up on the same type of paper at home. Some accommodations – like a computer or tablet – are a good tool for any child to have at home.

Keyboard skills are an integral part of almost any career; it's a skill that once learned, will benefit your child for life.

If your child is home-schooled, consult with an experienced occupational therapist, clinical psychologist and assistive technology specialist to design a plan that will best suit your child's needs.

Common Modifications and Accommodations

Modifications and accommodations depend on age and skill level. Not all of these modifications may be appropriate for your child. For example, a tablet or computer is good for older children while spacemen are for beginning writers.

Lined Paper or Graph Paper

This accommodation provides lined paper for every task instead of blank paper. Some lined paper has raised lines and colored lines that helps to keep the writing on the line and cues the student where they stop writing. Providing graph paper instead of lined paper can help the student put letters or numbers in the right place.

Spacing Paper

Spacing paper helps students transition from primary paper to wide ruled notepaper and teaches them correct spacing between letters. It also encourages children to write letters the correct size and increases legibility. The paper looks like normal notebook paper but has tick marks evenly spaced on the lines (similar to graph paper), so that children write one letter in each space. Mead brand offers spacing paper, called RediSpace.

Really Good Stuff's Spacemen

This kit, from the website ReallyGoodStuff.com helps children use proper spacing in their composition. Spacemen is a bucket of 30 spacemen that work instead of fingers. After repeated use, the goal is for students to place spaces naturally without the assistance of the tool.

Keyboards and other Assistive Devices

Keyboards and computers are part of modern life. Once we're out of school, nearly everyone uses a computer. Teaching your child computer skills and asking the school to provide a tablet or computer for writing in class can build confidence for a child who has trouble writing letters. Other assistive technologies that can help include talk-to-text software that can translate words to written text. If your child has an IEP, ask the school to provide your child with a keyboard. You might request that the IEP team and the teacher meet with you at the same time to discuss the issue.

Provide Classroom Notes

Usually, students take notes in class while the teacher is lecturing. This can place a heavy burden on a student with dysgraphia, as their concentration is with letter and word formation, not with what is being said. In addition, if the student's writing is illegible, they will be unable to refer back to their notes. To overcome this problem, teachers can provide students with lecture notes or partial notes, which allow the student to take *some* notes.

Give the student a scribe

A scribe is a note taker; they should write what the student says verbatim and make no changes. The student then reviews the work, makes oral corrections and the scribe rewrites the paper according to the student's directions. A scribe can be a friend, relative, or even you! Although school districts do not generally provide a scribe for a child with dysgraphia, some colleges and universities will, via the school's disability services office.

Motor Dysgraphia

With motor dysgraphia, an IEP or 504 plan is usually not necessary; you can take steps to help your child on your own or with the assistance from a teacher or occupational therapist for guidance.

One of the first steps you can take to help your child write correctly is by ensuring that they are holding the pencil the right way. The best or most effective way to hold a pencil is called a dynamic tripod grasp.

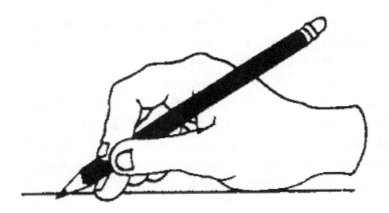

The tripod grasp

There are other ways to hold a pencil, and not all of those positions require intervention. For example, another way to effectively hold a pencil is the quadripod grasp. Quadripod is very similar to the tripod grasp: "Quadripod" means that four fingers are used, while "tripod" means that three fingers are used.

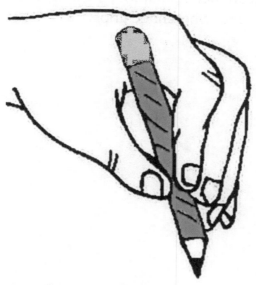

The quadripod grip

A third type of grip, the adaptive tripod (also called a D'Nealian grip), is also a functional way to hold a pencil. With this grasp, the pencil is held between the index finger and the third finger. The tips of the thumb and index finger rest on the pencil.

There are many pencil tools available on the market to help to achieve the ideal (a tripod grip), including a bulb gripper and Twist 'n write pencil. Pencil grips are not necessary before the age of about six. Before that age, children tend to use immature grasp patterns which evolve into a tripod grip. The first step in helping with motor dysgraphia is identifying how your child holds a pencil, then purchasing a tool to help with the type of grip. An occupational therapist can help you choose a correct grip, as there are many on the market. Here are some of the most common immature pencil-holding styles, along with the recommended grips:

1.   The supinate grasp

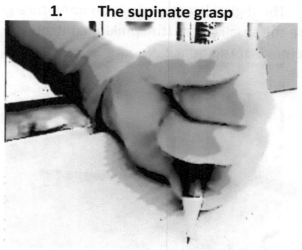

The supinate grasp is a crude grasp that involves the whole fist. It is commonly seen in very young children who have not yet reached school age. It's very rare to see children use this grasp once they are in school. The bulb gripper is a pencil attachment that can help very young children to grasp the pencil correctly.

A bulb gripper

2.   Digital brace grasp

The digital brace grasp is an immature grasp where the small finger (the pinkie) controls the movement of the pencil.

A Twist 'n write pencil can help a child with a digital brace grasp achieve the correct hold for a pencil.

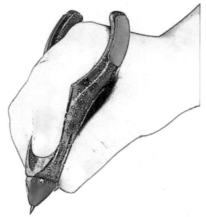

3.   Thumb wrap grasp

The thumb wrap grasp is easily identified because the thumb wraps all the way around the pencil.

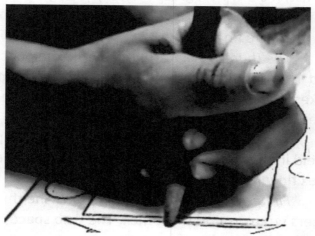

The thumb wrap grasp can be corrected with a grotto grip. The Grotto grip helps with correct thumb placement and promotes the tripod grip. It is rather bulky, so older children may be reluctant to use it in the classroom. This grip can be used by left or right-handed children.

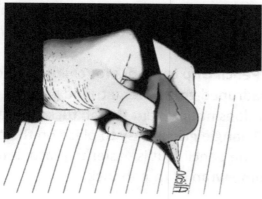

Other types of immature grasp include:

A fisted grasp: The pencil is held with the hand in a fist. It's a typical grasp for very young children.

A five finger grasp: The pencil is held with the tips of all five fingers.

The thumb tuck or thumb wrap: The pencil is held in a tripod or quadripod grasp but the thumb is tucked under the index finger or is wrapped over the index finger.

Tripod grasp with closed web space: The pencil is held in the tripod position but the web between the index finger and thumb is completely closed.

Finger wrap: The index finger and the third fingers wrap around the pencil. The web space is completely closed.

Other types of grip on the market can also help your child:

The Stetro grip is very small and inconspicuous. However, it can be confusing to use: the thumb is placed in the star and there are arrows to indicate finger placement for right-handers (down arrow) and left-handers (up-arrow).

The Pencil Grip can work for children who prefer a quadruped grasp over a tripod grasp. However, it does not prevent thumb tuck or wrap.

The Triangle grip is easy to place on the pencil and widens the pencil to it is easier to grasp. It doesn't prevent thumb wrap or thumb tuck.

The Cushion grip prevents children from grasping the pencil too tightly and so can help with joint pain. However, this type of grip does not help to correct finger or thumb placement and will not fix the problem of holding the pencil too tightly (it just provides a cushion).

Once you have selected the right gripper for your child, encourage your child to use it when writing or drawing. This may be difficult at first, as the change in pencil grasp may feel very strange and isn't what your child is comfortable with. After a month, remove the gripper and watch how your child grasps the pencil. If they have achieved a good grip (i.e. a tripod grasp) then discontinue use of the gripper. If there isn't a change, get your child to use the gripper for another month. In most cases, the gripper only needs to be used for a month or two until the child's muscle memory kicks in and they get used to the new hand placement. Muscle memory also makes a play in writing letters; when your child has the same grip each time, they write the letters of the alphabet the same way each time. Eventually the brain kicks in and makes letter writing an automatic process.

Hand strengthening
There are more than 25 muscles in the forearm and hand that control movement. Some larger muscles contribute more to certain activities like squeezing a ball. If a child can squeeze a ball really hard, it may look like they have strong hands, but

that's not the whole picture. What's just as important for writing or drawing is the smaller muscles in the hand. If those muscles are not developed, it may result in problems with coordination when trying to manipulate a pencil or pen, pick up small objects, fastening zippers, using scissors and other activities that require fine motor skills. Your child may benefit from hand strengthening activities to help them with their pencil grasp. Anything that provides resistance can help build the muscles in the hand:

- Clay, Play-Doh, Silly Putty, Bread Dough, or Plasticine are great materials for providing children with resistance exercises like pushing, pulling, flattening and molding.

- Interlocking construction toys like Mega Blocks, Legos, Tinker toys, K'Nex or Bristle blocks help to build fine motor muscles. Choose an appropriate age-level construction toy for your child.

- Spray bottles, squirt guns, sponges and other water toys that provide resistance can also help. Turkey basters and bulb syringes can also be used to squirt water. What child doesn't like to use a spray gun? These fun tools can help build fine motor muscles.

- Digging in the yard requires a surprising amount of fine motor skills.

- Cutting with scissors is a good way to develop hand muscles.

- Clothes pin games. Play a pick-up game with cotton balls, pompons, crumbled paper, beads and other small objects. Place different colors for each "team" and then see who can pick up the objects the fastest. One rule for the game: the clothespin should be squeezed open with the thumb and forefinger to build muscle strength. If you don't have any clothespins, connected chopsticks, tweezers or tongs can work as well.
- Hole puncher: use a hole puncher to punch out holes from paper. These can be used as confetti to make a picture.
- Dressing dolls: requires a surprising amount of finger work, especially for tiny outfits with lots of buttons or snaps.

Practice the Alphabet

Get your child to copy the upper case letters of the alphabet from a large-size sheet. The appendix of this book has the letters of the alphabet that are large enough for a child to copy. Encourage your child to practice every day for a month and then ask them to write the letters *without copying*. Use lined paper (such as in an elementary school comprehension book) so that your child can follow the lines of the letters. If they are successful, great! If not, practice for another week and repeat the process until they have learned the upper case letters. When they are able to write the upper case letters without copying, switch to lower case letters and repeat the technique. Continue until your child has learned the alphabet.

If your child still cannot write well after learning the correct grip and practicing the alphabet, it may be time to look at another reason for poor writing skills, like dyslexic dysgraphia. Ask your school district to re-evaluate your child, or ask a clinical psychologist for help.

Dyslexic Dysgraphia

Children with dyslexic dysgraphia have trouble with temporary memory and permanent memorization of words and letters. The type of "automatic" writing that most people can do does not come easily (if at all) to people with dyslexic dysgraphia. They can't form images of words and letters in their head; a child with dyslexic dysgraphia will be unable to write out the letters of the alphabet correctly with their eyes closed.

Some techniques you can try at home to help your child include helping them to learn the alphabet (as outlined in the previous section. You should also teach your child to type.

Break Writing Down into Steps

Writing an assignment can be an overwhelming task with many steps that can be hard to remember. When giving your child a writing assignment, encourage them to break the task down into smaller steps. The first step in writing any assignment is brainstorming ideas. Your child could use a small tape recorder or record their thoughts on a computer. Other options are creating a flow chart to organize thoughts, or writing the thoughts on note cards and organizing them. Next comes a rough draft, and then an edit of this rough draft to make sure there is a main idea and that each paragraph has a topic sentence. Finally, in the third draft, there's a grammar and spelling check. Make sure your child has a break in between each of these steps. In particular, have your child set aside the assignment and make a final edit a couple of days later. Even seasoned writers *without* dyslexic dysgraphia wait a couple of days to look at their work with fresh eyes.

Have a notebook handy with the steps written down so that your child can refer to the steps at any time. Focus only on one writing aspect for each assignment. Good writing has originality, a flow, a topic, good paragraph organization, grammar and spelling. When giving your child a writing assignment, focus only on one of these aspects to make the task seem less overwhelming.

Avoid Timed Tests

Don't give your child a specific time to finish an assignment. If you must give your child a timed assessment, don't criticize spelling or grammar. Focus instead on their ideas and content of the writing.

Software that Helps

There is a huge amount of software on the market available to help with dyslexic dysgraphia with an abundance of features. Which features your child needs is an individualized decision. Consider consulting with an occupational therapist or assisted technology specialist to make a decision about what software types can help your child. You can also ask your school about the types of software they have available so that you can purchase the same software for use at home. In general, all children with dyslexic dysgraphia will benefit from having software with these key features:

- Mind mapping/visual organizer
- Split screen feature
- Speech-to-text software
- Speech output (where the software reads what is on the screen out loud)
- Word predictor (much like the text predictions on smartphones)
- Dictionary and spell checker

You may need to purchase more than one product to obtain all of the features you need. Some good software products for children with dyslexia:

For-Fee Products

Mindmeister (online resource)
Mindmeister is an online mind-mapping tool. It's ideal for real-time collaboration. An additional feature is that you can integrate a Skype account into your profile. Each mind-map begins with a central idea in the middle of the screen. From there, you can add related concepts which can be rearranged with ease. Mindmeister also keeps track of revisions and the maps can be exported to a file or printed. The program is free for 30 days; after that you must pay $2.99 per month.

Inspiration/Kidspiration
Inspiration (for middle schoolers and up) and Kidspiration (for K-5 learners) are visual organizers, where students can brainstorm using images and symbols. A personalized visual organizer helps students break down assignments into small steps. It includes:

- A talking interface text-to-speech for students who are challenged with focusing on printed text.
- A word retrieval tool to find and choose words.
- A storyboard creation tool to illustrate the sequence of events in a story.
- Compatibility with word, so that fleshed-out outlines can be exported as a Word document.

- Dozens of pre-loaded templates, from creating comic strips to character analysis.

Kidspiration or Inspiration can be purchased for about $40 (as of May 2014). A free trial is available from www.Inspiration.com.

WYNN Literacy Software Solution
WYNN software was developed specifically for students with reading challenges and writing difficulties like dysgraphia. WYNN Wizard, which at the time of writing sells for about $1,000, includes:
- The ability to scan printed pages and convert them into text on the computer.
- Speech synthesis for the scanned text to be read aloud.
- Reading out loud feature for any document, PDF or web page.

You can purchase WYNN at http://www.freedomscientific.com/.

Kurzweil 3000
Kurzweil 3000 is a text-to-speech program that combines reading text from a computer with a range of study and language tools. It also includes an integrated voice notes feature and a "read the Web" tool to read web pages out loud. The software costs around $1400.

Free Products

Audacity Sound Recorder and Editor (downloadable program)

Audacity Sound Recorder and Editor is a free open source program that records live audio, converts tapes and records into digital recordings or CD's, edits MP3 and WAV files, and much more. Students can record using a microphone or keyboard.

Bruce's Unusual Typing Wizard (Downloadable Program)

This full featured and sophisticated, typing tutor offers introductory lessons, practice exercises, and games. Best for older children and adults. The program can be downloaded from http://typing.qcalculus.com/.

Bubbl.us

Bubbl.us is an online mind-mapping application for brainstorming. It's simple to use, with an easily understandable user interface. Bubbl.us also makes it possible to work collaboratively with other students online and share your work. The mind-map a student makes can be saved as an image file or printed for later use. The program is free and does have a few drawbacks compared to paid software: you can't import your own images, icons are not included for use in the maps and there isn't a drawing tool for free hand sketching.

CLiCk, Speak

This program reads aloud any web page in Firefox. Three mouse-activated buttons allow you to read selected text, begin reading wherever the cursor is placed, and stop reading. The program highlights each sentence as it is read. The extension can easily be added to the Firefox toolbar.

You can download the toolbar from http://clickspeak.clcworld.net/

Dragnifier

Dragnifier is a "quick dragging magnifier" for anything on your computer screen. Download the tool for free from Ed Halley's website:

http://www.halley.cc/stuff/dragnifier.html

e-Learning for Kids

This online tool is a set of drills, activities, and games to help children learn a variety of computer and keyboarding skills. It combines an engaging space and tournament theme.

Visit the site at:

http://www.e-learningforkids.org/computer-skills/

EverNote Free (downloadable program)

EverNote is a way to take and store notes in a variety of different formats. The notes can be organized by category. Templates are available for a variety of tasks like expenses, shopping lists, and phone messages.

Download athttp://www.evernote.com/en/

Free Mind (downloadable program)

Free Mind is another brainstorming, or mind-mapping software. Ideas and concepts can be graphically represented and turned into a mind map on screen. The user interface is easy to use and built-in keyboard commands provide access to virtually all program functions. The program is best suited for middle-school aged children and older.

To download Free Mind, go to http://freemind.sourceforge.net/wiki/index.php/Main _Page

Fx Software

This website that offers a variety of free downloadable assistive software. The titles include:

- **KwikLoupe** —a simple screen magnifier.
- **mmFollow** – adds a cartoon character to the mouse cursor.
- **Mouseketeer** — mouse clicking/dragging tool.
- **RapidSet** — allows you to change font and/or background color easily.

- **Sonar 4** — creates a permanent ring around the mouse pointer to make it easier to keep track of.
- **Vu-Bar 4** — tool for keeping a single line of text in view.

Visit the site at http://www.fx-software.co.uk/assistive.htm.

Mindomo

Mindomo is a full-featured online mind-mapping platform. The software enables you to:

- Customize the look of any mind map.
- Easily collapse or extend sub topics. Attach notes to topics or sub-topics.
- Easily share mind maps and collaborate online.
- Embed links to websites.
- Import images from the web.

Visit Mindmomo at: http://www.mindomo.com/

Mindomo mind maps can be exported in a variety of file formats.

One drawback: with the free "basic" version, you can only create one project and two mind maps.

ReadTheWords.com

ReadTheWords.com is an online text-to-speech service. You can enter text with the keyboard, copy and paste text, or upload text files from your computer or from other websites. You can listen to the text online, or download an mp3 file for use offline.

TheSage (downloadable program)
The Sage is a free dictionary and thesaurus program with an extensive vocabulary. One helpful feature is access to your ongoing history of word searches.
Download the program at http://www.sequencepublishing.com/index.html (This program runs in Windows.)

Speakonia (downloadable program)

This text-to-speech reader is built using Microsoft Speech Technology. Copy and paste text into the Speakonia interface and that text can be read to you. The program can also read out loud any highlighted text. You also have the option of saving text as audio wav files.

The program can also be used as an editing tool for writing. Type directly into the Speakonia interface and then hear it read what you have written. Files can be saved or copied and pasted into another program, like Word.

Get the program at: http://www.cfs-technologies.com/home/?id=1.4

Fox Splitter

This Firefox add-on allows you to view multiple open tabs on the same screen. A split browser can help a learner make comparisons when doing research. The add on is easy to use: split the browser with a right mouse click to open the context menu options. You can split the screen into as many windows as you wish. Download from: https://addons.mozilla.org/en-US/firefox/addon/fox-splitter-formerly-split-br/

Thinkature (online resource)

This online mind-mapping application is simple and easy to use. You can:

- Pile cards on top of each other

- Cluster cards together
- Connect cards
- Add graphics from your hard drive or the web
- Draw free hand with the drawing tool

Visit the site at:
http://www.makeuseof.com/tag/thinkature/

WikiMindMap (online resource)

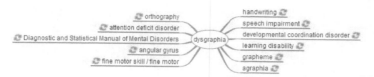

A sample map generated by typing "dysgraphia" into WikiMindMap.

This brainstorming software helps you to create your own mind maps and find and visually represent the links between concepts. Wikimindmap also gives you more information about any related concept. The default language is German, so make sure you select "en.wikipedia.org" from the home screen's drop-down menu to create a mind map.
Find the tool at:
http://www.wikimindmap.org/

Word Web (downloadable program) WordWeb is a free dictionary and thesaurus. Once the program is downloaded, click on an icon in your system tray to bring up the dictionary/thesaurus.

Download from http://wordweb.info/free/

YAKiToMe! Is an online text-to-speech service that allows you to enter text directly, input document files and receive input directly from email accounts. YAKiToMe! Audio files can be saved as either .wav or .mp3.

Visit the site: https://www.yakitome.com

Related Disorders

Dysgraphia often overlaps with other learning disabilities such as speech impairment, attention deficit disorder, or developmental coordination disorder.

Dyslexia, or **developmental reading disorder**, is characterized by difficulty with learning to read fluently and with accurate comprehension despite normal or above-average intelligence. This includes difficulty with phonological awareness, phonological decoding, processing speed, orthographic coding, auditory short-term memory, language skills/verbal comprehension, and/or rapid naming.

Dyslexia is the most common learning difficulty and most recognized reading disorder. There are other reading difficulties that are unrelated to dyslexia.

Some see dyslexia as distinct from reading difficulties resulting from other causes, such as a non-neurological deficiency with vision or hearing, or poor or inadequate reading instruction. There are three proposed cognitive subtypes of dyslexia (auditory, visual and attentional), although individual cases of dyslexia are better explained by specific underlying neuropsychological deficits and co-occurring learning difficulties (e.g. an auditory processing disorder, an attention deficit hyperactivity disorder, a visual processing disorder) and co-occurring learning difficulties (e.g. dyscalculia and dysgraphia).Although it is considered to be a receptive language-based learning disability in the research literature, dyslexia also affects one's expressive language skills. Researchers at MIT found that people with dyslexia exhibited impaired voice-recognition abilities. Interestingly, a study published online (and in the July issue of the American Journal of Human Genetics), reported a genetic origin to the disorder, and other learning disabilities, that could help lead to earlier diagnoses and more successful interventions.

Internationally, dyslexia has no single definition; more than 70 names are used to describe its manifestations, characterizations or causes. The World Federation of Neurology defines dyslexia as "a disorder manifested by difficulty in learning to read despite conventional instruction, adequate intelligence and sociocultural opportunity". The National Institute of Neurological Disorders and Stroke definition also adds, "difficulty with spelling, phonological processing (the manipulation of sounds), and/or rapid visual-verbal responding."Many published definitions from researchers and organizations around the world are purely descriptive or embody causal theories. These definitions for the disorder, defined as dyslexia, encompass a number of reading skills, deficits and difficulties with a number of causes rather than a single condition.

Signs and symptoms

In early childhood, early symptoms that correlate with a later diagnosis of dyslexia include delays in speech, letter reversal or mirror writing, difficulty knowing left from right and directions, and being easily distracted by background noise. This pattern of early distractibility is partially explained by the co-occurrence of dyslexia and attention-deficit/hyperactivity disorder. Although each disorder occurs in approximately 5% of children, 25–40% of children with either dyslexia or ADHD meet criteria for the other disorder.

Dyslexic children of school age can have various symptoms; including difficulty identifying or generating rhyming words, or counting syllables in words (phonological awareness), a difficulty segmenting words into individual sounds, or blending sounds to make words, a difficulty with word retrieval or naming problems, commonly very poor spelling, which has been called dysorthographia or dysgraphia, whole-word guesses, and tendencies to omit or add letters or words when writing and reading are considered classic signs.

Signs persist into adolescence and adulthood with trouble with summarizing a story, memorizing, reading aloud, and learning a foreign language. Adult dyslexics can read with good comprehension, although they tend to read more slowly than non-dyslexics and perform more poorly at spelling and nonsense word reading, a measure of phonological awareness.

A common misconception about dyslexia is that dyslexic readers write words backwards or move letters around when reading – this only occurs in a very small population of dyslexic readers. Individuals with dyslexia are better identified by reading accuracy, fluency, and writing skills that do not seem to match their level of intelligence from prior observations.

Oral and Written Language Learning Disability

OWL LD is a language disorder with the same impairments as dyslexia. In addition, children with OWL LD have problems with morphological and syntactic coding and comprehension. Morphology is the identification, analysis, and description of the structure of a given language's morphemes and syntax is how words and phrases are arranged to create sentences. Children with OWL LD may also have the same writing and reading and related disorders as children with dysgraphia or dyslexia.

Speech disorders

Speech disorders or speech impediments are a type of communication disorder where 'normal' speech is disrupted. This can mean stuttering, lisps, or other speech problems.

Classifying speech into normal and disordered is more problematic than it first seems. By a strict classification, only 5% to 10% of the population has a completely normal manner of speaking (with respect to all parameters) and a healthy voice; everyone else has one disorder or another.

- Stuttering affects approximately 1% of the adult population.
- Cluttering, a speech disorder that has similarities to stuttering.
- Dysprosody is the rarest neurological speech disorder. It is characterized by alterations in

intensity, in the timing of utterance segments, and in rhythm, cadence, and intonation of words. The changes to the duration, the fundamental frequency, and the intensity of tonic and atonic syllables of the sentences spoken, deprive an individual's particular speech of its characteristics. The cause of dysprosody is usually associated with neurological pathologies such as brain vascular accidents, cranioencephalic traumatisms, and brain tumors.

- Muteness is complete inability to speak
- Speech sound disorders involve difficulty in producing specific speech sounds (most often certain consonants, such as /s/ or /r/), and are subdivided into articulation disorders (also called phonetic disorders) and phonemic disorders. Articulation disorders are characterized by difficulty learning to produce sounds physically. Phonemic disorders are characterized by difficulty in learning the sound distinctions of a language, so that one sound may be used in place of many. However, it is not uncommon for a single person to have a mixed speech sound disorder with both phonemic and phonetic components.
- Voice disorders are impairments, often physical, that involve the function of the larynx or vocal resonance.
- Dysarthria is a weakness or paralysis of speech muscles caused by damage to the nerves

and/or brain. Dysarthria is often caused by strokes, Parkinson's disease, ALS, head or neck injuries, surgical accident, or cerebral palsy.

• Apraxia of speech may result from stroke or be developmental, and involves inconsistent production of speech sounds and rearranging of sounds in a word ("potato" may become "topato" and next "totapo"). Production of words becomes more difficult with effort, but common phrases may sometimes be spoken spontaneously without effort. It is now considered unlikely that childhood apraxia of speech and acquired apraxia of speech are the same thing, though they share many characteristics.

There are three different levels of classification when determining the magnitude and type of a speech disorder and the proper treatment or therapy:

1. Sounds the patient can produce.

1. Phonemic- can be produced easily; used meaningfully and contrastively.

2. Phonetic- produced only upon request; not used consistently, meaningfully, or contrastively; not used in connected speech.

2. Stimulable sounds

1. Easily stimulable.

2. Stimulable after demonstration and probing (i.e. with a tongue depressor).

3. Cannot produce the sound

1. Cannot be produced voluntarily.

2. No production ever observed.

Causes

In many cases the cause is unknown. However, there are various known causes of speech impediments, such as hearing loss, neurological disorders, brain injury, intellectual disabilities, drug abuse, physical impairments such as Cleft lip and palate, and vocal abuse or misuse. Child abuse may also be a cause in some cases.

Treatment

Many of these types of disorders can be treated by speech therapy, but others require medical attention by a doctor in phoniatrics. Other treatments include correction of organic conditions and psychotherapy.

In the United States, school-age children with a speech disorder are often placed in special education programs. More than 700,000 of the students served in the public schools' special education programs in the 2000-2001 school year were categorized as having a speech or language impediment. This estimate does not include children who have speech/language problems secondary to other conditions such as deafness". Many school districts provide the students with speech therapy during school hours, although extended day and summer services may be appropriate under certain circumstances.

Patients will be treated in teams, depending on the type of disorder they have. A team can include; SLP's, specialists, family doctors, teachers, and parents/family members.

Social effects

Suffering from a speech disorder can have negative social effects, especially among young children. Those with a speech disorder can be targets of bullying because of their disorder. The bullying can result in decreased self-esteem. Later in life, bullying is experienced less by a general population, as people become more understanding as they age.

Language disorders are usually considered distinct from speech disorders, even though they are often used synonymously.

Speech disorders refer to problems in producing the sounds of speech or with the quality of voice, where language disorders are usually an impairment of either understanding words or being able to use words and does not have to do with speech production.

ADHD predominantly inattentive

ADHD predominantly inattentive (ADHD-PI or ADHD-I) is one of the three subtypes of Attention-deficit hyperactivity disorder (ADHD). While ADHD-PI is sometimes still called "attention deficit disorder" (ADD) by the general public, these older terms were formally changed in 1994 in the new Diagnostic and Statistical Manual of Mental Disorders, fourth edition (DSM-IV).

Differences from other ADHD subtypes

ADHD-PI is similar to the other subtypes of ADHD in that it is characterized primarily by inattention, easy distractibility, disorganization, procrastination, and forgetfulness; where it differs is in lethargy - fatigue, and having fewer or no symptoms of hyperactivity or impulsiveness typical of the other ADHD subtypes. In some cases, children who enjoy learning may develop a sense of fear when faced with structured or planned work, especially long or group-based that requires extended focus, even if they thoroughly understand the topic. Children with ADHD-PI may be at greater risk of academic failures and early withdrawal from school. Teachers and parents may make incorrect assumptions about the behaviors and attitudes of a child with ADHD-PI, and may provide them with frequent and erroneous negative feedback (e.g. "you're irresponsible", "you're immature", "you're lazy", "you don't care/show any effort", "you just aren't trying", etc.).

The inattentive children may realize on some level that they are somehow different internally from their peers. However, they are also likely to accept and internalize the continuous negative feedback, creating a negative self-image that becomes self-reinforcing. If these children progress into adulthood undiagnosed or untreated, their inattentiveness, ongoing frustrations, and poor self-image frequently create numerous and severe problems maintaining healthy relationships, succeeding in postsecondary schooling, or succeeding in the workplace. These problems can compound frustrations and low self-esteem, and will often lead to the development of secondary pathologies including anxiety disorders, sexual promiscuity, mood disorders, and substance abuse.

It has been suggested that some of the symptoms of ADHD present in childhood appear to be less overt in adulthood. This is likely due to an adult's ability to make cognitive adjustments and develop coping skills minimizing the frequency of inattentive or hyperactive behaviors. However, the core problems of ADHD do not disappear with age. Some researchers have suggested that individuals with reduced or less overt hyperactivity symptoms should receive the ADHD-combined diagnosis. Hallowell and Ratey (2005) suggest that the manifestation of hyperactivity simply changes with adolescence and adulthood, becoming a more generalized restlessness or tendency to fidget.

In the DSM-III, sluggishness, drowsiness, and daydreaming were listed as characteristics of ADHD. The symptoms were removed from the ADHD criteria in DSM-IV because, although those with ADHD-PI were found to have these symptoms, this only occurred with the absence of hyperactive symptoms. These distinct symptoms were described as sluggish cognitive tempo (SCT).

A meta-analysis of 37 studies on cognitive differences between those with ADHD-Inattentive type and ADHD-Combined type found that "the ADHD/C subtype performed better than the ADHD/I subtype in the areas of processing speed, attention, performance IQ, memory, and fluency. The ADHD/I subtype performed better than the ADHD/C group on measures of flexibility, working memory, visual/spatial ability, motor ability, and language. Both the ADHD/C and ADHD/I groups were found to perform more poorly than the control group on measures of inhibition, however, there was no difference found between the two groups. Furthermore the ADHD/C and ADHD/I subtypes did not differ on measures of sustained attention."

Some experts, such as Dr. Russell Barkley, argue that ADHD-PI is so different from the other ADHD subtypes that it should be regarded as a distinct disorder. ADHD-PI is noted for the almost complete lack of conduct disorders and high-risk, thrill-seeking behavior, and additionally have higher rates of anxiety. Further research needs to be done to discover differences among those with attention disorders.

Symptoms

DSM-IV criteria

The DSM-IV allows for diagnosis of the predominantly inattentive subtype of ADHD (under code 314.00) if the individual presents six or more of the following symptoms of inattention for at least six months to a point that is disruptive and inappropriate for developmental level:

- Often does not give close attention to details or makes careless mistakes in schoolwork, work, or other activities.
- Often has trouble keeping attention on tasks or play activities.
- Often does not seem to listen when spoken to directly.
- Often does not follow instructions and fails to finish schoolwork, chores, or duties in the workplace (not due to oppositional behavior or failure to understand instructions).
- Often has trouble organizing activities.
- Often avoids, dislikes, or doesn't want to do things that take a lot of mental effort for a long period (such as schoolwork or homework).

- Often loses things needed for tasks and activities (e.g. toys, school assignments, pencils, books, or tools).
- Is often easily distracted.
- Is often forgetful in daily activities.
- Often mixes up peoples' names or forgets them for short periods of time.

An ADHD-PI diagnosis is contingent upon the symptoms of impairment presenting themselves in two or more settings (e.g., at school or work and at home). There must also be clear evidence of clinically significant impairment in social, academic, or occupational functioning. Lastly, the symptoms must not occur exclusively during the course of a pervasive developmental disorder, schizophrenia, or other psychotic disorder, and are not better accounted for by another mental disorder (e.g., mood disorder, anxiety disorder, dissociative disorder, personality disorder).

Examples of observed symptoms

Life Period Example

Children

Failing to pay close attention to details or making careless mistakes when doing school-work or other activities.

Trouble keeping attention focused during play or tasks.

Appearing not to listen when spoken to (often being accused of "daydreaming").

Failing to follow instructions or finish tasks.

Avoiding tasks that require a high amount of mental effort and organization, such as school projects.

Frequently losing items required to facilitate tasks or activities, such as school supplies.

Excessive distractibility.

Forgetfulness.

Procrastination, inability to begin an activity.

Adults

Often making careless mistakes when having to work on uninteresting or difficult projects.

Often having difficulty keeping attention during work, or holding down a job for a significant amount of time.

Often having difficulty concentrating on conversations.

Having trouble finishing projects that have already been started.

Often having difficulty organizing for the completion of tasks.

Avoiding or delaying in starting projects that require a lot of thought.

Often misplacing or having difficulty finding things at home or at work.

Disorganized personal items (sometimes old and useless to the individual) causing excessive "clutter" (in the home, car, etc.).

Often distracted by activity or noise.

Often having problems remembering appointments or obligations, or inconveniently changing plans on a regular basis.

Prevalence in children

It is difficult to say exactly how many children worldwide have ADHD because different countries have used different ways of diagnosing it, while some do not diagnose it at all. In the UK, diagnosis is based on quite a narrow set of symptoms, and about 0.5–1% of children are thought to have attention or hyperactivity problems. In comparison, until recently, professionals in the USA used a much broader definition of the term ADHD.

As a result, up to 10% of children in the USA were described as having ADHD. Current estimates suggest that ADHD is present throughout the world in about 1–5% of the population. About five times more boys than girls are diagnosed with ADHD. This may be partly because of the particular ways they express their difficulties. Boys and girls both have attention problems, but boys are more likely to be overactive and difficult to manage. Children from all cultures and social groups are diagnosed with ADHD. However, children from certain backgrounds may be particularly likely to be diagnosed with ADHD, because of different expectations about how they should behave. It is therefore important to ensure that a child's cultural background is understood and taken into account as part of the assessment.

Treatment

Recent studies indicate that medications approved by the U.S. Food and Drug Administration (FDA) in the treatment of ADHD tend to work well in individuals with the predominantly inattentive type. These medications include two classes of drugs: stimulants and non-stimulants. Drugs for ADHD are divided into first-line medications and second-line medications. First-line medications include several of the stimulants, and tend to have a higher response rate and affect size than second-line medications. Some of the most common stimulants are Methylphenidate (Ritalin, Concerta), Adderall and Vyvanse. Second-line medications are usually anti-depressant medications such as Zoloft, Prozac, and Wellbutrin. These medications can help with fidgeting, inattentiveness, irritability, and trouble sleeping. Some of the symptoms the medications target are also found with ADHD-PI patients.

Although medication can help improve concentration, it does not cure ADHD-I and the symptoms will come back once the medication stops.

Medication works better for some patients while it barely works for others.

Along with medication, behavioral therapy is recommended to improve organizational skills, study techniques or social functioning.

Strategies for parents

Parents are recommended to learn about this disorder in order to first be able to help themselves and then their children.

Behavioral strategies are of great help and they include creating routines, getting organized, avoiding distractions, limiting choices, using goals and rewards, and ignoring behaviors.

Children with ADHD can be extremely disorganized. Parents should work with them to find specific places for everything and teach kids to use calendars and schedules. Parents are advised to get children into sports to help them build discipline, confidence, and improve their social skills. Physical activity boosts the brain's dopamine, norepinephrine, and serotonin levels and all these neurotransmitters affect focus and attention. Some sports may be too challenging and would add frustration. Parents should talk with their children about what activities and exercises most stimulate and satisfy them before signing them up for classes or sports.

It is important to establish close communication with the school in order to develop an educational plan to address the child's needs. Accommodations in school, such as extended time for tests or more frequent feedback from teachers, are beneficial for these individuals.

Developmental dyspraxia

Developmental dyspraxia is a chronic Neurological disorder beginning in childhood that can affect planning of movements and co-ordination as a result of brain messages not being accurately transmitted to the body. It may be diagnosed in the absence of other motor or sensory impairments like cerebral palsy, muscular dystrophy, multiple sclerosis or Parkinson's disease.

Dyspraxia is a specific learning difficulty (SpLD) so it does not affect overall intelligence or ability, but just affects particular aspects of development. The concept of developmental dyspraxia has existed for more than a century, but differing interpretations of the terminology remain.

The Dyspraxia Foundation defines developmental dyspraxia as "an impairment or immaturity of the organization of movement. It is an immaturity in the way that the brain processes information, which results in messages not being properly or fully transmitted. The word 'dyspraxia' comes from the Greek words 'dys', meaning impaired or abnormal, and 'praxis', meaning action or deed.

Dyspraxia affects the planning of what to do and how to do it. It is associated with problems of perception, language and thought". Dyspraxia is described as having two main elements:

- deational dyspraxia: difficulty with planning a sequence of coordinated movements.
- deo-Motor dyspraxia: difficulty with executing a plan, even though it is known.

Ripley, Daines, and Barrett state that "Developmental dyspraxia is difficulty getting our bodies to do what we want when we want them to do it", and that this difficulty can be considered significant when it interferes with the normal range of activities expected for a child of their age.

Epidemiology

Developmental dyspraxia (referred to as developmental coordination disorder in the US and Europe) is a life-long neurological condition that is more common in males than in females, with a ratio of approximately four males to every female. The exact proportion of people with the disorder is unknown since the disorder can be difficult to detect due to a lack of specific laboratory tests, thus making diagnosis of the condition one of elimination of all other possible causes/diseases. Current estimates range from 5%–20% with 5–6% being the most frequently quoted percentage in the literature. Some estimates show that up to 1 in 30 children may have dyspraxia.

Assessment and diagnosis

Assessments for dyspraxia typically require a developmental history, detailing ages at which significant developmental milestones, such as crawling and walking, occurred. Motor skills screening includes activities designed to indicate dyspraxia, including balancing, physical sequencing, touch sensitivity, and variations on walking activities. A baseline motor assessment establishes the starting point for developmental intervention programs. Comparing children to normal rates of development may help to establish areas of significant difficulty.

However, research in the British Journal of Special Education has shown that knowledge is severely limited in many who should be trained to recognize and respond to various difficulties, including Developmental Coordination Disorder, Dyslexia and DAMP. The earlier that difficulties are noted and timely assessments occur, the quicker intervention can begin. A teacher or GP could miss a diagnosis if they are only applying a cursory knowledge.

"Teachers will not be able to recognise or accommodate the child with learning difficulties in class if their knowledge is limited. Similarly GPs will find it difficult to detect and appropriately refer children with learning difficulties."

Developmental profiles

Various areas of development can be affected by developmental dyspraxia and these will persist into adulthood, as dyspraxia has no cure. Often various coping strategies are developed, and these can be enhanced through occupational therapy, physiotherapy, speech therapy, or psychological training.

Speech and language

Developmental verbal dyspraxia is a type of ideational dyspraxia, causing linguistic or phonological impairment. This is the favored term in the UK; however it is also sometimes referred to as articulatory dyspraxia and in the United States the usual term is childhood apraxia of speech (CAS). Key problems include:

- Difficulties controlling the speech organs.
- Difficulties making speech sounds.
- Difficulty sequencing sounds.
- Within a word.
- Forming words into sentences.
- Difficulty controlling breathing and phonation.
- Slow language development.
- Difficulty with feeding.

Fine motor control

Difficulties with fine motor co-ordination lead to problems with handwriting, which may be due to either ideational or ideo-motor difficulties. Problems associated with this area may include:

- Learning basic movement patterns.
- Developing a desired writing speed.

- The acquisition of graphemes – e.g. the letters of the Latin alphabet, as well as numbers.
- Establishing the correct pencil grip.
- Hand aching while writing.

Fine-motor problems can also cause difficulty with a wide variety of other tasks such as using a knife and fork, fastening buttons and shoelaces, cooking, brushing one's teeth, applying cosmetics, styling one's hair, opening jars and packets, locking and unlocking doors, shaving and doing housework.

Whole body movement, coordination, and body image

Issues with gross motor coordination mean that major developmental targets including walking, running, climbing and jumping can be affected. The difficulties vary from child to child and can include the following:

- Poor timing.
- Poor balance (sometimes even falling over in mid-step). Tripping over one's own feet is also common.
- Difficulty combining movements into a controlled sequence.
- Difficulty remembering the next movement in a sequence.
- Problems with spatial awareness, or proprioception.
- Some people with dyspraxia have trouble picking up and holding onto simple objects

such as picking pencils and things up, owing to poor muscle tone and or proprioception.

- This disorder can cause an individual to be clumsy to the point of knocking things over and bumping into people accidentally.
- Some people with dyspraxia have difficulty in determining left from right.
- Cross-laterality, ambidexterity, and a shift in the preferred hand are also common in people with dyspraxia.
- People with dyspraxia may also have trouble determining the distance between them and other objects.

General difficulties

In addition to the physical impairments, dyspraxia is associated with problems with memory, especially short-term memory. This typically results in difficulty remembering instructions, difficulty organizing one's time and remembering deadlines, increased propensity to lose things or problems carrying out tasks which require remembering several steps in sequence (such as cooking.) Whilst most of the general population experiences these problems to some extent, they have a much more significant impact on the lives of dyspraxic people. However, many dyspraxics have excellent long-term memories, despite poor short-term memory. Many dyspraxics benefit from working in a structured environment, as repeating the same routine minimizes difficulty with time-management and allows them to commit procedures to long-term memory.

People with dyspraxia may have sensory processing disorder, including abnormal oversensitivity or undersensitivity to physical stimuli, such as touch, light, and sound. This may manifest itself as an inability to tolerate certain textures such as sandpaper or certain fabrics and including oral toleration of excessively textured food (commonly known as picky eating), or even being touched by another individual (in the case of touch oversensitivity) or may require the consistent use of sunglasses outdoors since sunlight may be intense enough to cause discomfort to a dyspraxic (in the case of light oversensitivity). An aversion to loud music and naturally loud environments (such as clubs and bars) is typical behavior of a dyspraxic individual who suffers from auditory oversensitivity, while only being comfortable in unusually warm or cold environments is typical of a dyspraxic with temperature oversensitivity. Undersensitivity to stimuli may also cause problems. Dyspraxics who are under sensitive to pain may injure themselves without realizing. Some dyspraxics may be oversensitive to some stimuli and under sensitive to others. These are commonly associated with autism spectrum conditions.

People with dyspraxia sometimes have difficulty moderating the amount of sensory information that their body is constantly sending them, so as a result these people are prone to panic attacks. Having other autistic traits (which is common with dyspraxia and related conditions) may also contribute to sensory-induced panic attacks.

Dyspraxia can cause problems with perception of distance, and with the speed of moving objects and people. This can cause problems moving in crowded places and crossing roads and can make learning to drive a car extremely difficult or impossible.

Many dyspraxics struggle to distinguish left from right, even as adults, and have extremely poor sense of direction generally.

Moderate to extreme difficulty doing physical tasks is experienced by some dyspraxics, and fatigue is common because so much extra energy is expended while trying to execute physical movements correctly. Some (but not all) dyspraxics suffer from hypotonia, which in this case is chronically low muscle tone caused by dyspraxia. People with this condition can have very low muscle strength and endurance (even in comparison with other dyspraxics) and even the simplest physical activities may quickly cause soreness and fatigue, depending on the severity of the hypotonia. Hypotonia may worsen a dyspraxic's already poor balance.

Overlap with other conditions

Dyspraxics may have other difficulties that are not due to dyspraxia itself but often co-exist with it. This is sometimes referred to as comorbidity. Dyspraxics may have characteristics of dyslexia (difficulty with reading and spelling), dyscalculia (difficulty with mathematics), expressive language disorder (difficulty with verbal expression), ADHD (poor attention span and impulsive behavior, which up to 50% of dyspraxics may have.), or Asperger syndrome (consisting variously of poor social cognition, a literal understanding of language [making it hard to understand idioms or sarcasm] and rigid, intense interests). However, they are unlikely to have problems in all of these areas. The pattern of difficulty varies widely from person to person, and it is important to understand that a major weakness for one dyspraxic can be a strength or gift for another. For example, while some dyspraxics have difficulty with reading and spelling due to an overlap with dyslexia, or numeracy due to an overlap with dyscalculia, others may have brilliant reading and spelling or mathematical abilities, however many dyspraxics also struggle with math. Some estimates show that up to 50% of dyspraxics may have ADHD.

Students with Dyspraxia struggle most in visual-spatial memory. When compared to their peers who don't have motor difficulties, students with dyspraxia are seven times more likely than typically developing students to achieve very poor scores in visual-spatial memory. As a result of this working memory impairment, students with dyspraxia have learning deficits as well.

Some Students with dyspraxia can also have comorbid language impairments. Research has found that students with dyspraxia and normal language skills still experience learning difficulties despite relative strengths in language. This means that for students with dyspraxia their working memory abilities determine their learning difficulties. Any strength in language that they have is not able to sufficiently support their learning.

Other names

Collier first described developmental dyspraxia as 'congenital maladroitness'. A. Jean Ayres referred to it as a disorder of sensory integration in 1972 while in 1975 Dr Sasson Gubbay called it the 'clumsy child syndrome'. It has also been called minimal brain dysfunction although the two latter names are no longer in use. Other names include:

- Dyspraxia.
- Developmental Co-ordination Disorder (DCD) - a subtly different condition by definition, in practice, very similar.
- Sensorimotor dysfunction.
- Perceptuo-motor dysfunction.
- Motor Learning Difficulties.

The World Health Organization currently lists Developmental Dyspraxia as Specific Developmental Disorder of Motor Function.

Appendix

TEACHERS AND PARENTS CHECKLIST FOR CLASSROOM RECOGNITION OF A CHILD WITH LANGUAGE AND LEARNING DIFFERENCE

Present this completed checklist to your child's teacher or other professional to aid with the diagnosis of dysgraphia or a related disorder:

Name of Student:_____

Date of Birth:_____

Grade:_____

School:_____

Put an X next to each one that applies:

Unable to read satisfactorily in spite of adequate intelligence and educational opportunity

Work does not reflect intellectual ability.

Unusual difficulty in handwriting.

Unusual difficulty in spelling (beyond the weekly spelling test).

Unable to recite the alphabet in sequence.

Unable to write the alphabet in sequence.

Reversals, rotations, transpositions, in reading and writing.

Directional confusion: left-right, before-after, over-under.

Poor recall ability, especially for names and words.

Poor auditory discrimination or confusion with

similar speech sounds.

Unable to copy accurately from the near point, far point, or both.

No definite preference for right or left hand.

Difficulty following directions.

Forgets assignments and/or loses papers.

Lacks organizational skills.

Short attention span.

Overly active and disturbing in classroom.

Unusually passive and withdrawn.

Inconsistent: Knows the material some days and doesn't remember it on other days.

A downward trend in achievement scores can be noted.

Source:
www.dyslexiacenterofutah.org

Alphabet Practice

Photocopy the following pages and give them to your child to help with alphabet practice. The first sheet is for smaller children who are just learning to write. The second sheet is for children who are learning to write the alphabet. Practice for about ten minutes a day should be all that is necessary (until your child has learned the alphabet and can write it out with their eyes closed).

A	B	C	D
E	F	G	H
I	J	K	L
M	N	O	P
Q	R	S	T
U	V	W	X
Y	Z		

A B C D E F G H I

J K L M N O P Q R

S T U V W X Y Z

a b c d e f g h i j k l m

n o p q r s t u v w y z

Mazes and Dot-to-Dots

Mazes and dot-to-dot pictures are excellent ways for small children to learn fine motor control. You can find maze and dot-to-dot books at educational stores and major book retailers.

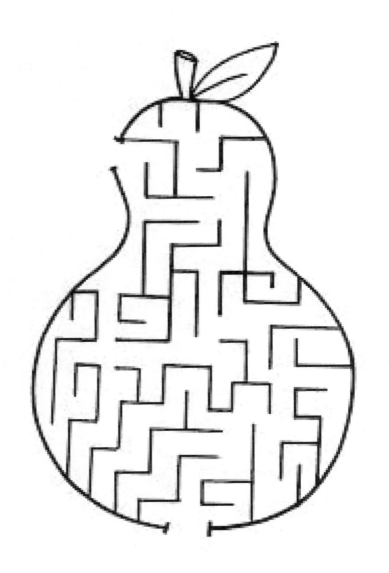

This maze is tricky. Can you make it to the end?

Start

End

Start

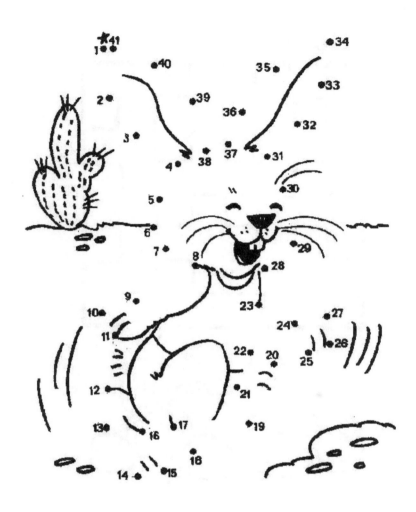

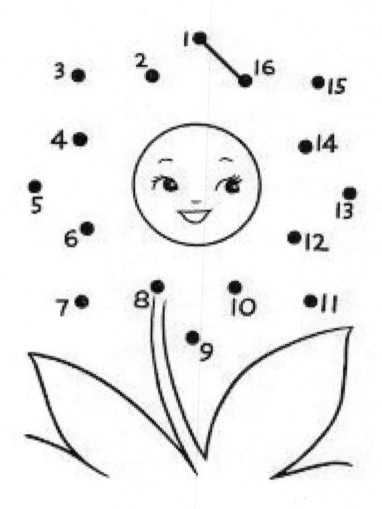

Glossary

504 plan: a reference to Section 504 of the Rehabilitation Act of 1973; Provide accommodations for some children with disabilities if they do not qualify for an EIP.

Accommodations means to reduce the impact writing has on the student, without substantially changing the assignment or process.

Adaptive tripod grip: see D'Nealian grip

Assistive Technology Specialist: a person who provides service to help people with disabilities choose and use assistive technology devices like specialized computer software.

Clinical Psychologist: Clinical Psychologists assess, diagnose, treat and prevent mental disorders.

D'Nealian grip: the pencil is held between the index finger and the third finger. The tips of the thumb and index finger rest on the pencil.

Developmental dyspraxia: a chronic Neurological disorder beginning in childhood that can affect planning of movements and co-ordination as a result of brain messages not being accurately transmitted to the body.

Digital brace grasp: an immature grasp where the small finger (the pinkie) controls the movement of the pencil.

Dysgraphia is a learning disability that affects the ability to write.

Dyslexia: a learning disability that features impaired word decoding and spelling.

Dyslexic Dysgraphia: A person with dyslexic dysgraphia (sometimes called processing dysgraphia) can copy text, color and draw close to normal. However, spelling words out loud (oral spelling) is below age level and written text is illegible.

Motor Dysgraphia: A person with motor dysgraphia can color, draw and paint within normal boundaries but has trouble with all written work, included copied work. Caused by poor fine motor skills.

Hereditary condition: a condition that is genetic. In other words, it runs in the family.

IEP: see individualized education plan.

Individualised Education Plan: a program that ensures a school child with an identified disability under the law receives specialized education services such as occupational therapy.

Intellectual disability: limitations with mental functioning and in skills like communication or taking care of themselves.

Legible: readable writing

Modifications: means a change to the **assignments** or expectations according to the student's needs.

Occupational Therapist: a person who works with a client to help them achieve a fulfilled and satisfied state in life through the use of "purposeful activity or interventions designed to achieve functional outcomes which promote health, prevent injury or disability and which develop, improve, sustain or restore the highest possible level of independence."(AOTA)

Oral and Written Language Learning Disability: OWL LD is a language disorder with the same impairments as dyslexia. In addition, children with OWL LD have problems with morphological and syntactic coding and comprehension.

Orthographic coding: refers to the ability to store unfamiliar written words (along with the language rules) in temporary or permanent memory. Orthographic loop: part of the working memory that integrates the letters and written words in the mind's eye with hand and finger movements needed for writing.

Orthography: the way language is written. It includes the rules for spelling, grammar, punctuation, hyphenation, word breaks and capitalization.

Phonological loop: the part of the brain that deals with sound or phonological information.

Processing dysgraphia: see dyslexic dysgraphia.

Quadripod grip: A four finger grip.

School Psychological Examiners: assessors who work with students in public schools, interviewing, observing, and administering and interpreting standardized testing instruments that measure cognitive and academic abilities.

Scribe: a note taker:

SLD: selective language disorder.

Spaceman: a tool to help children use proper spacing in their composition.

Spacing Paper: The paper looks like normal notebook paper but has tick marks evenly spaced on the lines (similar to graph paper), so that children write one letter in each space.

Spatial dysgraphia: This type of dysgraphia is caused by the brain having problems with evaluating what the eyes are seeing and how objects are positioned relative to each other.

Special Education Teacher: a person who educates children with special needs like learning disabilities.

Supinate grasp: a crude grasp that involves the whole fist.

Thumb wrap grasp: the thumb wraps all the way around the pencil.

Tripod grip: a three finger grip.

Visual organizer: a tool that uses visual symbols to express knowledge, concepts, thoughts, or ideas, and the relationships between them.

References

Adams, M. J. (1981). What good is orthographic redundancy? In O. J. L. Tzeng & H. Singer (Eds.),
AOTA Inc., 1994, p.1073

Apel, K. (2009). The acquisition of mental orthographic representations for reading and spelling

B.A. O'Brien et al.Therrien, W. J. (2004). Fluency and comprehension gains as a result of repeated reading. Remedial and Special Education, 25, 252–261.

Balmuth, M. (2009). The roots of phonics. A historical introduction (Revised ed.). Baltimore, MD: Paul H. Brookes.

Balmuth, M. (2009). The roots of phonics. A historical introduction (Revised ed.).Baltimore, MD: Paul H. Brookes.

Berninger, V. (2008). Evidence-based written language instruction during early and middle childhood. In R. Morris & N. Mather (Eds.), Evidence-based interventions for students with learning and behavioral challenges. Philadelphia: Lawrence Erlbaum Associates.

Berninger V., Richards T. (2010). Inter-relationships among behavioral markers, genes, brain, and treatment in dyslexia and dysgraphia. Future Neurol. 5, 597–617.10.2217/fnl.10.22

Berninger, V., & Wolf, B. (2009a). Teaching students with dyslexia and dysgraphia: Lessons from teaching and science. Baltimore, MD: Paul H. Brookes.

Berninger, V., O'Donnell, L., & Holdnack, J. (2008). Research-supported differential diagnosis of specific learning disabilities and implications for instruction and response to instruction (RTI). In A. Prifitera, D. Saklofske, & L. Weiss (Eds.), WISC-IV Clinical Assessment and Intervention, Second Edition (pp. 69–108). San Diego, CA: Academic Press (Elsevier).

Hinshelwood J. (1907). Four cases of congenital word-blindness occurring in the same family. Br. Med. J. 2, 1229–1232.

Lyon (Ed.), Frames of reference for the assessment of learning disabilities: New views on measurement issues (pp. 279–329). Baltimore: Paul H. Brookes.

Rayner, K., Foorman, B. R., Perfetti, C. A., Pesetsky, D., & Seidenberg, M. S. (2001). How psychological science informs the teaching of reading. Psychological Science in the Public Interest, 2(2), 31–74.

Reitsma, P. (1983). Printed word learning in beginning readers. Journal of Experimental Child Psychology, 36(2), 321–339.

Roach, N. W., & Hogben, J. H. (2004). Attentional modulation of visual processing in adult dyslexia: A spatial-cuing deficit. Psychological Science, 15(10), 650–654.

Saklofske, & L. Weiss (Eds.), WISC-IV Clinical Assessment and Intervention, Second Edition (pp. 69–108). San Diego, CA: Academic Press (Elsevier).

Stanovich, K. E., & West, R. F. (1989). Exposure to print and orthographic processing. Reading ResearchQuarterly, 24(4), 402–433.

Stephenson S. (1907). Six cases of congenital word-blindness affecting three generations of one family. Opthalmoscope 5, 482–484

Sunseth, K., & Bowers, P. G. (2002). Rapid naming and phonemic awareness: Contributions to reading,spelling, and orthographic knowledge. Scientific Studies of Reading, 6, 401–429.

Tabachnick, B. G., & Fidell, L. S. (1989). Using multivariate statistics. New York: Harper Collins Publishers. 134

Torgesen, J. K., Wagner, R. K., & Rashotte, C. A. (1999). Test of word reading efficiency. Examiner's manual. Austin: PRO-ED.

Treiman, R. (1997). Spelling in normal children and dyslexics. In B. Blachman (Ed.), Foundations of reading acquisition and dyslexia: Implications for early intervention (pp. 191–219). Mahwah: Erlbaum.

Vellutino, F. R., Scanlon, D. M., & Tanzman, M. S. (1994). Components of reading ability: Issues and problems in operationalizing word identification, phonological coding, and orthographic coding. In G. R.

Speech_impairment

Pinto JA, Corso RJ, Guilherme AC, Pinho SR, Nóbrega Mde O (March 2004). "Dysprosody nonassociated with neurological diseases--a case report". J Voice18 (1): 90–6.doi:10.1016/j.jvoice.2003.07.005. PMID 15070228.

"Disability Info: Speech and Language Disorders Fact Sheet (FS11)." National Dissemination Center for Children with Disabilities.http://www.nichcy.org/pubs/factshe/fs11txt.htm

http://www.lbfdtraining.com/Pages/emt/sectiond/childabuse.htmlLong Beach (California) Fire Department

"Speech Defect." Encyclopedia.com.http://www.encyclopedia.com/doc/1E1-speechde.html

Disability Info: Speech and Language Disorders Fact Sheet (FS11)

http://en.wikipedia.org/wiki/Speech_impairment

Deputy, Paul; Human Communication Disorders; March 10, 2008

Attention_deficit_disorder

Quinn, Patricia (1994). ADD and the College Student: A Guide for High School and College Students with Attention Deficit Disorder. New York, NY: Magination Press. pp. 2–3. ISBN 1-55798-663-0.

Triolo, Santo (1998). Attention Deficit Hyperactivity Disorder in the hood: A Practitioner's Handbook. Philadelphia, PA: Brunner-Routledge. pp. 65–69. ISBN 0-87630-890-6.

Kelly, Kate; Peggy Ramundo (2006). You Mean I'm Not Lazy, Stupid or Crazy?! The Classic Self-Help Book For Adults with Attention Deficit Disorder. New York, NY: Scribner. pp. 11–12. ISBN 0-7432-6448-7.

Hallowell, Edward M.; John J. Ratey (2005). Delivered from Distraction: Getting the Most out of Life with Attention Deficit Disorder. New York: Ballantine Books. pp. 253–5. ISBN 0-345-44231-8.

Lane, B. (2004). The differential neuropsychological/cognitive profiles of ADHD subtypes: A meta-analysis. Dissertation Abstracts

International, 64, Retrieved from PsycINFO database.

Barkley, Russell A. (2001). "The Inattentive Type of ADHD As a Distinct Disorder: What Remains To Be Done". Clinical Psychology: Science and Practice 8 (4): 489–501. doi:10.1093/clipsy/8.4.489.

Milich, Richard; Balentine, Amy C., Lynam, Donald R.. "ADHD Combined Type and ADHD Predominantly Inattentive Type Are Distinct and Unrelated Disorders". Clinical Psychology: Science and Practice 8 (4): 463–488.doi:10.1093/clipsy/8.4.463.

Murphy, K., Barkley, R., & Bush, T. (2002). Young adults with attention deficit hyperactivity disorder: subtype differences in comorbidity, educational, and clinical history. The Journal Of Nervous And Mental Disease, 190(3), 147-157. Retrieved from MEDLINE database.

Bauermeister, J., Matos, M., Reina, G., Salas, C., Martínez, J., Cumba, E., et al. (2005). Comparison of the DSM-IV combined and inattentive types of ADHD in a school-based sample of Latino/Hispanic children. Journal Of Child Psychology And Psychiatry, And Allied Disciplines, 46(2), 166-179. Retrieved from MEDLINE database.

What we know National Resource Centre on AD/HD

WHO adult AD/HD inattentive symptoms [1] National Resource Center on ADHD

"What is ADD". Retrieved 2011-01-10.

"ADHD treament can take on a range of types and methods.". Retrieved 2010-04-08.

Pharmaceutical treatments for ADHD-Medications. Retrieved 2011-04-09

"Are ADHD Drugs Right for You or Your Child?". Retrieved 2010-04-08.

"Inattentive AD/HD: Overlooked and Undertreated?". Retrieved 2010-04-08.

"ADHD Fact Sheet". Retrieved 2010-04-08.

"The Best Summer Sports for ADHD Kids". Retrieved 2010-04-08.

"Ten Tips for the Parents of an ADHD Inattentive Child". Retrieved 2010-04-08.

"AD/HD Predominantly Inattentive Type (WWK8)". Retrieved 2010-04-08.

http://en.wikipedia.org/wiki/Attention_deficit_disorder

Dyspraxia

http://alifewithdyspraxia.webs.com/whatisdyspraxia.htm

http://www.nldontheweb.org/librarybooks/relateddisorders.html

http://en.wikipedia.org/wiki/List_of_neurological_disorders

"Dyspraxia Info". Retrieved April 2010.

Scope UK

muscular-dystrophy.org

Henderson, SE; Henderson, L (2003). "Toward an understanding of developmental coordination disorder: terminological and diagnostic issues". Neural Plast 10 (1–2): 1–13. doi:10.1155/NP.2003.1.PMC 2565424.PMID 14640303.

"Terminology used in research reports of developmental coordination disorder. Lívia C Magalhães. 2007; Developmental Medicine & Child Neurology - Wiley InterScience".

Dewey, D (1995). "What is developmental dyspraxia?".Brain Cogn 29 (3): 254–74.doi:10.1006/brcg.1995.1281.PMID 8838385.

http://www.dyspraxiafoundation.org.uk/services/dys_dyspraxia.php

Jenny Barrett, Kate Ripley, Bob Daines (1997). Dyspraxia: A Guide For Teachers and Parents (Resource Materials for Teachers). David Fulton Publishers, Ltd. pp. 3. ISBN 1-85346-444-9.

The Dyspraxia Support Group of New Zealand. "What is dyspraxia?". Retrieved 2008-04-05.

Gaines, Robin; Cheryl Missiuna , Mary Egan, Jennifer McLean (2008-01-22). "Educational outreach and collaborative care enhances physician's perceived knowledge about Developmental Coordination Disorder". BMC Health Services Research 8: 21.doi:10.1186/1472-6963-8-21.PMC 2254381.PMID 18218082. Retrieved 2011-07-20.

Kirby, Amanda; Davies, Rhys; Bryant, Amy (2005-11). Do teachers know more about specific learning difficulties than general practitioners?. British Journal of Special Education

Pam Williams, Developmental Verbal Dyspraxia, Nuffield Hearing & Speech Centre

http://www.dyspraxiafoundation.org.uk/services/ad_symptoms.php

http://www.chichesterprimarytutors.co.uk/specific-learning-difficulties/dyspraxia/

Biggs, Victoria (2005). "2 The Hidden People at Home".Caged in chaos : a dyspraxic guide to breaking free. London ; Philadelphia: Jessica Kingsley Publishers.ISBN 9781843103479.

http://www.dyspraxiafoundation.org.uk/services/gu_symptoms.php

Biggs, Victoria (2005). "1 A Recipe for Chaos". Caged in chaos : a dyspraxic guide to breaking free. London ; Philadelphia: Jessica Kingsley Publishers.ISBN 9781843103479.

Biggs, Victoria (2005). "3 A Survival Guide to School".Caged in chaos : a dyspraxic guide to breaking free. London ; Philadelphia: Jessica Kingsley Publishers.ISBN 9781843103479.

http://www.bicpa.ac.uk/gdg/dyspraxia.html

http://www.dyspraxiafoundation.org.uk/services/ad_employers.php

Biggs, Victoria "Caged in Chaos" Chapter X Jessica Kingsley 2005

"Dyspraxia". Retrieved 2008-04-05.

http://www.livingwithcerebralpalsy.com/hypotonia-cerebral.php

http://www.remspeced.co.za/Articles/20071101_0002.htm

NINDS, information on hypotonia

"Amanda Kirby speaking on the co-occurrence of learning difficulties". dysTalk. Retrieved 2009-04-22.

"Dyspraxia Adults Action". Retrieved 2008-04-05.

Alloway, TP (2007). "Working Memory, Reading and Mathematical Skills in Children with Developmental Coordination Disorder". Journal of Experimental Child Psychology96 (1): 20–36.doi:10.1016/j.jecp.2006.07.002.PMID 17010988.

Alloway, TP; Temple, K (2007). "A Comparison of Working Memory Profiles and Learning in Children with Developmental Coordination Disorder and Moderate Learning Difficulties".Applied Cognitive Psychology 21(4): 473–487.doi:10.1002/acp.1284.

Alloway, TP; Archibald, L (2008). "Working Memory and Learning in Children with Developmental Coordination Disorder and Specific Language Impairment".Journal of Learning Disabilities 41(3): 251–62.doi:10.1177/0022219408315815. PMID 18434291.

Irvine, Chris (2008-08-17)."Harry Potter's Daniel Radcliffe has dyspraxia". The Daily Telegraph (London). Retrieved 2010-05-16.

Salmon, Mary (2003-06-30)."Dyspraxia is no bar to success". The Times (London). Retrieved 2010-05-16.

Paphides, Pete (2009-06-19)."What's haunting Florence and the Machine?". The Times(London). Retrieved 2010-05-16.

Smith, Andrea (2009-03-15)."Hannah: You're not wrong and you're not broken". Irish Independent. Retrieved 2011-11-03.

"What does it mean to be dyspraxic?". Retrieved 2010-05-16.

"Einstein and Newton had Autism". BBC News. 2003-04-30. Retrieved 2010-05-16.

"Library: Dysphasia / Dyspraxia". Retrieved 2010-05-16.

"Famous people with dyspraxia I". Retrieved 2010-05-16.

Biggs, Victoria "Caged in Chaos" Chapter 1 Page 18 Jessica Kingsley 2005

http://en.wikipedia.org/wiki/Developmental_coordination_disorder

Index

504 plan, 15, 16, 26, 30, 98

Accommodations, 17, 27, 71, 98

Adaptive tripod. See D'Nealian grip

ADHD, 55, 62, 63, 64, 65, 66, 68, 69, 70, 79, 108, 109, 110

Alphabet, 18, 39, 85

Assistive Devices, 28

Assistive Technology Specialist, 14, 98

Block letter writing, 18

Bulb gripper, 31, 33

Clinical Psychologist, 13, 98

Concept Map, 23

Cursive writing, 18

D'Nealian grip, 31, 98, 99

Developmental dyspraxia, 71, 72, 99

Diagnosis, 7

Digital brace grasp, 34

Dyslexia, 10, 11, 42, 54, 55, 56, 57, 78, 100, 104, 105, 106

Dyslexic Dysgraphia, 3, 11, 40, 99

Dyspraxia, 71, 78, 79, 80, 110, 111, 112, 113

Fisted grasp, 36

Hand strengthening, 37

Hereditary, 10

IEP, 15, 16, 26, 28, 30, 99

Intellectual disability, 5

Mazes, 25, 88

Mind mapping, 23

Modifications, 17, 27, 100

Motor Dysgraphia, 3, 12, 30, 99

Occupational Therapist, 14, 100

Oral and written language learning disability, 10, 35, 100

Orthographic, 8, 9, 10, 11, 18, 54, 104, 106

Orthographic coding, 9, 100

OWL LD, , See Oral and Written Language Learning Disability

Quadripod grip, 31

School Psychological Examiners, 13, 101

Scribe, 29

Software, 20, 23, 41, 43, 47
Spacemen, 28
Spacing paper, 27
Spatial dysgraphia, 12, 101
Special Education Teacher, 14, 101
Speech disorders, 57, 61
Supinate grasp, 33
Thumb tuck, 36
Thumb wrap grasp, 35
Treatment, 3, 17, 26, 60, 69
Tripod grasp, 30, 36, 37
Twist 'n write, 31
Visual organizer, 20, 22, 42, 43
Web space, 36

Made in United States
Troutdale, OR
01/02/2024

16625676R00066